This Book Belongs to

©2018

All rights Reserved

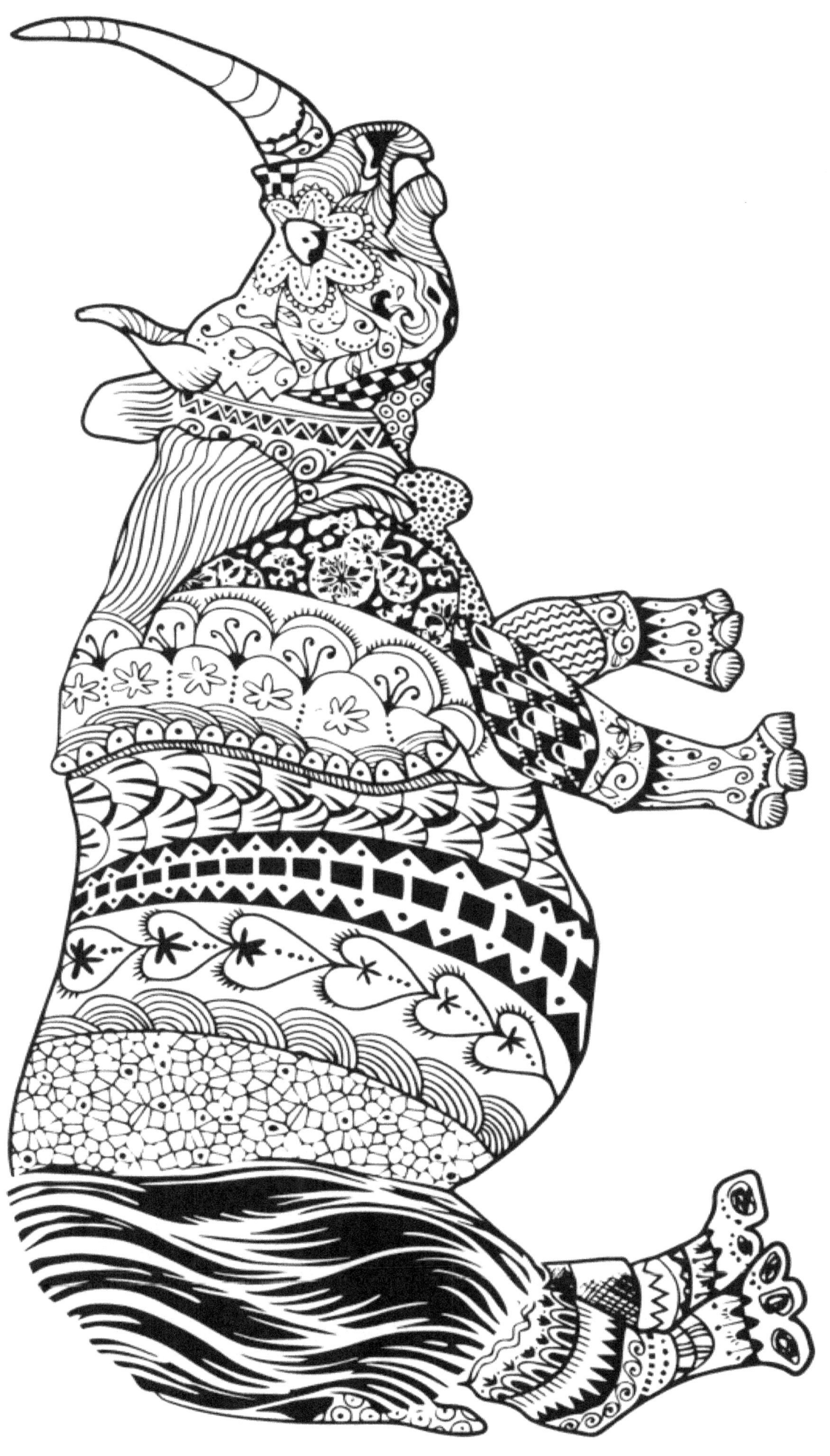

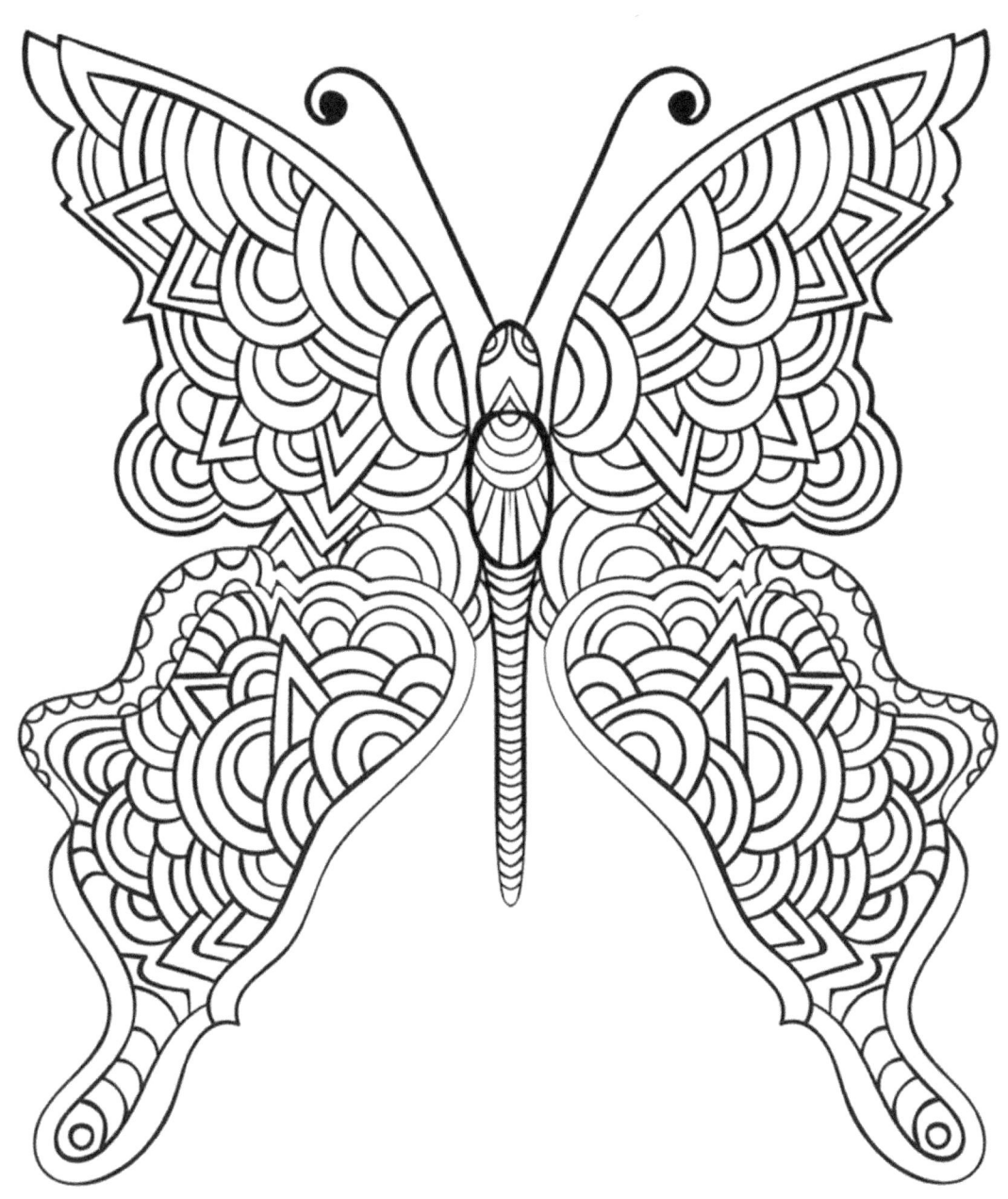

www.ingramcontent.com/pod-product-compliance
Lightning Source LLC
Chambersburg PA
CBHW082119220526
45472CB00009B/2244